REVERSE PSYCHOLOGY

Discovering how to interpret body language, assess emotions and actions, decode intentions, Manipulations and grasp motivations

By

Selena H. Hall

DISCLAIMER

Copyright © by Selena H. Hall 2024.

All rights reserved.

This document may not be replicated or reproduced in any form without permission from the publisher. As a result, the information inside cannot be transferred, stored electronically, or maintained in a database. The publisher or creator must give their consent before any part of the document may be copied, scanned, faxed, or stored.

TABLE OF CONTENT

Sandra, a recent college graduate, found herself facing stiff competition in the job market.

Determined to stand out, she devised a clever plan using **Reverse Psychology** during her interviews.

Instead of trying to impress potential employers with her qualifications, **Sandra** subtly downplayed her skills and experiences, presenting herself as humble and eager to learn.

During one interview, when asked about her strengths, **Sandra** replied modestly, "Well, I'm still learning and growing, but I've been told I have a knack for problem-solving and a strong work ethic."

Her humility and openness piqued the interviewer's interest, prompting them to delve deeper into her background and aspirations.

As the interview progressed, **Sandra** strategically highlighted her willingness to take on new challenges and her enthusiasm for the company's mission.

By reframing her lack of experience as an opportunity for growth and development, **Sandra** positioned herself as a valuable asset rather than a liability.

In the end, **Sandra**'s **Reverse Psychology** paid off. Impressed by her honesty, humility, and genuine enthusiasm, the interviewer offered her the job on the spot.

Through her clever use of **Reverse Psychology**, **Sandra** not only secured employment but also demonstrated the power of authenticity and humility in achieving success.

INTRODUCTION

In the intricate landscape of human interaction, where motives are often obscured and outcomes uncertain, lies the fascinating realm of **Reverse Psychology**. It is a subtle yet powerful tool—a psychological sleight of hand that defies conventional wisdom and challenges our perceptions of influence and persuasion.

Imagine a scenario where the direct approach proves ineffective, where conventional strategies falter in the face of resistance. It is here that **reverse psychology** emerges as a beacon of ingenuity—a strategic manoeuvre that operates in the realm of paradox and contradiction.

At its core, reverse psychology hinges on the art of manipulation in reverse—a strategic dance of suggestion and subtlety designed to elicit desired behaviours or outcomes by encouraging the opposite. It is a delicate balancing act, requiring finesse and foresight to navigate the complexities of human psychology.

Consider the parent who, frustrated by a child's defiance, employs **reverse psychology** to pique their curiosity and spur cooperation. Or the savvy marketer who, recognizing consumers' aversion to overt persuasion, subtly positions a product as exclusive or elusive, triggering a surge in demand.

Yet, **reverse psychology** is not without its risks and ethical considerations. Its potency lies in its ability to exploit cognitive biases and emotional triggers, raising questions of manipulation and authenticity. As such, its judicious use demands a nuanced understanding of human behavior and a commitment to integrity and transparency.

Embark with us on a journey through the captivating landscape of **reverse psychology**, where every twist and turn offers new insights into the complexities of human behavior. Together, we'll explore the principles that underpin this enigmatic phenomenon, delving into the depths of the human psyche to uncover the hidden forces that shape our thoughts and actions.

As we navigate this intriguing terrain, we'll encounter a myriad of real-world examples that illustrate the transformative power of **reverse psychology**. From interpersonal dynamics to marketing strategies, from parenting techniques to negotiation tactics, the applications of **reverse psychology** are as diverse as they are impactful.

But our exploration goes beyond mere observation—we invite you to become an active participant in the journey. Through thought-provoking exercises and engaging discussions, we'll challenge you to rethink your assumptions, question your instincts, and expand your understanding of influence and persuasion.

Along the way, we'll confront the ethical dilemmas inherent in the practice of **reverse psychology**, grappling with questions of manipulation, autonomy, and responsibility. We'll examine the boundaries between persuasion and coercion, exploring how to wield the power of influence with integrity and empathy.

Ultimately, our aim is not only to inform but to empower—to equip you with the knowledge and skills needed to navigate the complexities of human interaction with confidence and compassion.

Whether you're a parent seeking to motivate your child, a business leader looking to inspire your team, or simply a curious observer of the human condition, our journey into the world of **reverse psychology** promises to be a rewarding and enlightening one.

CHAPTER 1
Understanding Reverse Psychology

Understanding reverse psychology is akin to unlocking a hidden treasure chest of human behavior—a complex tapestry woven from the threads of **motivation**, **perception**, and **persuasion**.

At its essence, reverse psychology is a strategic maneuver that capitalizes on the paradoxical nature of human cognition, leveraging subtle suggestions and unexpected cues to elicit desired behaviors or outcomes.

Central to the concept of reverse psychology is the recognition that humans possess a natural inclination to resist direct coercion or manipulation.

When faced with overt persuasion, individuals often exhibit reactance—a psychological phenomenon characterized by a heightened resistance to perceived threats to freedom or autonomy.

In such instances, attempts to influence behavior through traditional means may prove counterproductive, triggering a defensive response that undermines the desired outcome.

Enter reverse psychology—a cunning approach that circumvents resistance by appealing to the innate desire for autonomy and control. Rather than issuing commands or directives, practitioners of reverse psychology employ subtle cues and strategic framing to nudge individuals toward the desired outcome indirectly.

By presenting options in a way that suggests autonomy and choice, rather than coercion or obligation, reverse psychology encourages voluntary compliance while preserving the individual's sense of agency.

Consider, for example, a parent attempting to persuade a stubborn child to eat their vegetables. Instead of resorting to threats or coercion, the parent might employ reverse psychology by framing the situation as a choice: **"It's up to you whether you want to eat your broccoli now or save it for later."** By granting the child a sense of control over the decision-making process, the parent taps into their natural inclination to assert autonomy, increasing the likelihood of cooperation.

Similarly, in the realm of marketing and advertising, reverse psychology is often deployed to influence consumer behavior subtly. Rather than employing overt sales tactics or aggressive persuasion techniques, savvy marketers leverage the principles of reverse psychology to create an aura of exclusivity or scarcity around a product or service.

By positioning an item as elusive or limited in availability, marketers capitalize on consumers' fear of missing out (FOMO), driving demand and fostering a sense of urgency to purchase.

Yet, the effectiveness of reverse psychology hinges not only on the artful manipulation of perception but also on a deep understanding of human psychology and behavior.

Successful practitioners of reverse psychology possess a keen awareness of cognitive biases, emotional triggers, and social dynamics, allowing them to craft messages and strategies that resonate with their target audience.

However, the practice of reverse psychology is not without its ethical considerations. While it can be a powerful tool for influencing behavior, it also has the potential to exploit vulnerabilities and manipulate individuals for personal gain. As such, its judicious use demands a commitment to transparency, honesty, and respect for the autonomy of others.

In conclusion, understanding reverse psychology requires a nuanced appreciation of the intricacies of human cognition and behavior. It is a delicate dance of perception and persuasion, where subtle cues and strategic framing are wielded to circumvent resistance and elicit voluntary compliance.

Whether employed in parenting, marketing, or interpersonal communication, reverse psychology offers a compelling framework for influencing behavior while respecting the autonomy and dignity of others.

CHAPTER 2
The Psychology Behind Reverse Tactics

The **psychology behind reverse tactics** delves deep into the intricate workings of the **human mind**, unraveling the mysteries of **motivation, perception**, and **persuasion**. At its core, reverse psychology harnesses the power of paradox—an intriguing interplay between conscious and unconscious processes that shape our thoughts, feelings, and behaviors in unexpected ways.

Central to the psychology behind reverse tactics is the concept of reactance—a fundamental aspect of human cognition characterized by a heightened resistance to perceived threats to freedom or autonomy.

When individuals feel coerced or manipulated, they often experience reactance as a defensive response, seeking to assert their independence and autonomy in the face of external influence.

Understanding this innate resistance to direct persuasion is crucial to the effectiveness of reverse tactics. Rather than confronting resistance head-on, practitioners of reverse psychology capitalize on the paradoxical nature of reactance by framing their messages or requests in a way that suggests autonomy and choice. By presenting options as suggestions rather than commands, they circumvent resistance and encourage voluntary compliance while preserving the individual's sense of agency.

The psychology behind reverse tactics also involves a sophisticated understanding of cognitive biases and heuristics—mental shortcuts that influence our decision-making processes.

By exploiting these biases, practitioners of reverse psychology can subtly shape perceptions and preferences, nudging individuals toward the desired outcome without arousing suspicion.

One such cognitive bias frequently leveraged in reverse tactics is the scarcity heuristic, which leads individuals to assign greater value to items or opportunities that are perceived as scarce or limited in availability. By framing a product or service as exclusive or in high demand, marketers can create a sense of urgency and desire, driving demand and increasing the likelihood of purchase.

Another powerful cognitive bias at play in reverse tactics is the anchoring effect, which occurs when individuals rely too heavily on the first piece of information encountered (the "anchor") when making decisions.

By strategically framing information or choices, practitioners of reverse psychology can anchor individuals' perceptions in a way that predisposes them toward the desired outcome.

Yet, the psychology behind reverse tactics extends beyond cognitive biases to encompass emotional triggers and social dynamics. Emotions play a central role in decision-making, influencing our perceptions, preferences, and actions in profound ways.

By tapping into emotions such as fear, desire, or curiosity, practitioners of reverse psychology can evoke powerful responses that motivate behavior change.

Furthermore, social dynamics play a crucial role in the effectiveness of reverse tactics. Social proof—the tendency to look to others for guidance in uncertain situations—can be leveraged to reinforce desired behaviors or preferences. By highlighting social norms or peer endorsements, practitioners of reverse psychology can create a sense of consensus and conformity that encourages compliance.

The psychology behind reverse tactics offers a fascinating glimpse into the complexities of human cognition and behavior.

By understanding the interplay between **reactance**, **cognitive biases**, **emotions**, and **social dynamics**, practitioners of reverse psychology can craft messages and strategies that resonate with their target audience, driving behavior change and influencing outcomes in subtle yet profound ways.

CHAPTER 3
Strategies and Techniques of
Reverse Psychology

Strategies and **techniques** of reverse psychology encompass a diverse array of approaches aimed at influencing behavior, shaping perceptions, and achieving desired outcomes through subtle suggestion and strategic framing.

From interpersonal interactions to marketing campaigns, practitioners of reverse psychology employ a nuanced toolkit of strategies designed to navigate the complexities of human cognition and behavior.

One of the central strategies of reverse psychology involves the artful framing of messages and requests in a way that appeals to individuals' sense of autonomy and choice. Rather than issuing commands or directives, practitioners present options as suggestions, allowing individuals to feel a sense of control over their decisions.

This approach taps into the natural inclination to resist coercion or manipulation, encouraging voluntary compliance while preserving the individual's sense of agency.

Another key technique of reverse psychology is the strategic use of scarcity and exclusivity. By framing a product or service as limited in availability or exclusive to a select few, practitioners can create a sense of urgency and desire that drives demand.

This leverages the scarcity heuristic—a cognitive bias that leads individuals to assign greater value to items or opportunities perceived as scarce or elusive.

Similarly, practitioners of reverse psychology often employ the anchoring effect—a cognitive bias that occurs when individuals rely too heavily on the first piece of information encountered.

By strategically anchoring individuals' perceptions in a way that predisposes them toward the desired outcome, practitioners can shape preferences and decisions in subtle yet powerful ways.

Emotions also play a crucial role in the strategies and techniques of reverse psychology. By tapping into emotions such as **fear**, **desire**, or **curiosity**, practitioners can evoke powerful responses that motivate behavior change. Whether through compelling storytelling, evocative imagery, or provocative messaging, emotions can be used to create a sense of urgency or desire that spurs action.

Social dynamics provide another fertile ground for the application of reverse psychology strategies. By leveraging social proof—the tendency to look to others for guidance—practitioners can reinforce desired behaviors or preferences.

Peer endorsements, testimonials, or social norms can be used to create a sense of consensus and conformity that encourages compliance.

Furthermore, practitioners of reverse psychology often employ the technique of strategic silence or reverse questioning. Rather than directly asserting a position or argument, they may withhold information or pose questions that lead individuals to arrive at the desired conclusion on their own.

This approach capitalizes on the power of suggestion and allows individuals to feel a sense of ownership over their decisions.

In summary, the strategies and techniques of reverse psychology offer a comprehensive toolkit for influencing behavior and shaping perceptions in subtle yet profound ways.

From framing messages to leveraging cognitive biases, emotions, and social dynamics, practitioners of reverse psychology navigate the complexities of human cognition and behavior with finesse and ingenuity.

By understanding and applying these strategies effectively, they can achieve their objectives while preserving the autonomy and dignity of those they seek to influence.

CHAPTER 4

Ethical Considerations in Implementing Reverse Psychology

Ethical considerations in implementing reverse psychology are paramount, as the practice involves influencing individuals' thoughts, behaviors, and decisions in ways that may have profound implications for their autonomy and well-being.

While reverse psychology can be a powerful tool for achieving desired outcomes, practitioners must navigate a delicate balance between persuasion and manipulation, ensuring that their strategies uphold principles of **integrity**, **transparency**, and **respect** for individuals' autonomy.

One of the primary ethical considerations in implementing reverse psychology is transparency. Practitioners must be honest and forthright about their intentions, ensuring that individuals are aware of the tactics being employed and the potential effects on their decisions.

Failure to disclose the use of reverse psychology can undermine trust and erode the integrity of the interaction, leading to feelings of manipulation or exploitation.

Practitioners must consider the potential impact of their strategies on individuals' autonomy and decision-making processes.

While reverse psychology aims to encourage voluntary compliance by presenting options as suggestions rather than commands, practitioners must be mindful of the power dynamics at play and avoid coercion or undue influence.

Individuals should feel free to make choices based on their preferences and values, without feeling pressured or manipulated.

Another ethical consideration in implementing reverse psychology is the potential for unintended consequences. While practitioners may have noble intentions in seeking to influence behavior for positive outcomes, they must consider the broader implications of their actions.

Strategies that rely on manipulation or exploitation of cognitive biases may inadvertently harm individuals' well-being or undermine their ability to make informed decisions.

Moreover, practitioners must consider the potential for harm when employing reverse psychology techniques, particularly in vulnerable populations or sensitive contexts.

Strategies that evoke strong emotions or exploit individuals' insecurities may have unintended negative effects on their mental health and emotional well-being.

Practitioners must exercise caution and sensitivity in their approach, prioritizing the dignity and welfare of those they seek to influence.

In addition, practitioners must be mindful of cultural differences and social norms when implementing reverse psychology strategies. What may be acceptable or effective in one cultural context may be perceived as unethical or inappropriate in another.

Practitioners must take into account the cultural backgrounds and values of their target audience, ensuring that their strategies are respectful and culturally sensitive.

Ultimately, ethical considerations in implementing reverse psychology require practitioners to approach their work with humility, empathy, and a commitment to not harm. While the practice offers opportunities for influencing behavior and achieving positive outcomes, practitioners must remain vigilant in safeguarding the autonomy, dignity, and well-being of those they seek to influence.

By adhering to principles of transparency, respect, and cultural sensitivity, practitioners can harness the power of reverse psychology ethically and responsibly, fostering trust and mutual respect in their interactions.

CHAPTER 5
Practical Applications in Daily Life

Practical applications of reverse psychology in daily life offer individuals a powerful resource kit for navigating interpersonal interactions, managing conflicts, and achieving desired outcomes with finesse and subtlety.

From parenting and relationships to negotiations and decision making, the principles of reverse psychology can be applied in a variety of contexts to influence behavior and shape perceptions effectively.

One of the most common applications of reverse psychology in daily life is in parenting. Parents often find themselves grappling with stubbornness or defiance from their children, and traditional approaches to discipline may prove ineffective or counterproductive.

By employing reverse psychology techniques, parents can encourage cooperation and compliance while preserving their child's sense of autonomy and independence. For example, rather than issuing directives or ultimatums, parents can present choices as suggestions, allowing children to feel a sense of control over their decisions.

Similarly, reverse psychology can be a valuable tool in managing relationships and interpersonal dynamics. In situations where direct communication fails to resolve conflicts or misunderstandings, subtle persuasion tactics can be employed to encourage empathy, understanding, and compromise.

By reframing perspectives and presenting options as suggestions, individuals can foster open dialogue and mutual respect, strengthening their relationships and resolving conflicts more effectively.

In the world of decision-making, reverse psychology can be used to overcome indecision or procrastination and motivate action. Individuals often struggle with inertia or fear of failure when faced with difficult choices or challenging tasks.

By presenting decisions as opportunities for growth and framing challenges as manageable obstacles, individuals can overcome self-doubt and take decisive action toward their goals.

Moreover, reverse psychology can be a powerful tool in influencing consumer behavior and shaping market trends. In an age of information overload and advertising saturation, consumers are increasingly skeptical of overt persuasion tactics and traditional marketing strategies.

By employing reverse psychology techniques, marketers can create a sense of exclusivity or scarcity around a product or service, driving demand and fostering brand loyalty.

For example, limited-time offers or exclusive discounts can create a sense of urgency and desire, motivating consumers to make a purchase.

In negotiations and conflict resolution, reverse psychology can be used to gain leverage and achieve favorable outcomes. Rather than adopting a confrontational or adversarial stance, negotiators can employ subtle persuasion tactics to influence their counterparts' perceptions and preferences.

By framing concessions as strategic moves or presenting alternatives as preferred options, negotiators can foster a spirit of cooperation and reach mutually beneficial agreements.

In conclusion, practical applications of reverse psychology in daily life offer individuals a versatile toolkit for influencing behavior, managing conflicts, and achieving desired outcomes with finesse and subtlety. From parenting and relationships to decision-making and negotiations, the principles of reverse psychology can be applied in a variety of contexts to navigate the complexities of human interaction and shape perceptions effectively.

By harnessing the power of persuasion and preserving individuals' autonomy and dignity, practitioners of reverse psychology can foster positive outcomes and strengthen relationships in all aspects of daily life.

CHAPTER 6
Reverse Psychology in Marketing and Advertising

Reverse psychology in marketing and advertising represents a sophisticated approach to influencing consumer behavior by appealing to innate psychological tendencies and biases.

In an era where consumers are increasingly savvy and skeptical of traditional marketing tactics, reverse psychology offers marketers a powerful strategy for capturing attention, driving engagement, and ultimately, increasing sales.

At its core, reverse psychology in marketing involves presenting products or services in a way that triggers a subtle yet powerful psychological response in consumers.

Rather than employing overt persuasion tactics or aggressive sales pitches, marketers leverage the principles of reverse psychology to create a sense of exclusivity, scarcity, or curiosity that motivates consumers to take action.

One of the most common applications of reverse psychology in marketing is the use of scarcity tactics. By framing products or promotions as limited in availability or exclusive to a select few, marketers create a sense of urgency and desire that drives demand. Limited-time offers, flash sales and exclusive discounts capitalize on consumers' fear of missing out (FOMO), prompting them to act quickly to secure the desired item or opportunity.

Similarly, reverse psychology can be employed through the use of social proof—the tendency to look to others for guidance in uncertain situations.

Testimonials, user reviews, and endorsements from influencers or celebrities serve as powerful forms of social proof that validate consumers' decisions and reinforce their confidence in a product or brand.

By leveraging social dynamics in this way, marketers can build trust and credibility with their target audience, increasing the likelihood of conversion.

Furthermore, reverse psychology can be applied through the strategic use of pricing and positioning. Marketers may intentionally price a product higher than its competitors to create the perception of higher quality or exclusivity—a phenomenon known as price anchoring.

By anchoring consumers' perceptions in this way, marketers can influence their preferences and willingness to pay, driving sales and maximizing profitability.

In addition to pricing, the language and imagery used in marketing materials can also be strategically crafted to evoke specific emotional responses in consumers.

By tapping into emotions such as **desire**, **nostalgia**, or **fear**, marketers can create a deeper connection with their audience and elicit a more visceral response to their messaging.

For example, ads that highlight the fear of missing out on a limited-time offer or the nostalgia of childhood memories can be particularly effective in driving engagement and conversion.

However, ethical considerations are paramount in the application of reverse psychology in marketing and advertising. While these tactics can be highly effective in influencing consumer behavior, they must be used responsibly and transparently to avoid manipulation or exploitation.

Marketers must ensure that their messaging is honest and truthful and that consumers are fully informed about the products or services being promoted.

Reverse psychology in marketing and advertising represents a powerful yet nuanced approach to influencing consumer behavior in today's competitive marketplace. By leveraging psychological principles such as **scarcity**, **social proof**, and **emotional resonance**, marketers can create compelling campaigns that capture attention, drive engagement, and ultimately, drive sales.

However, ethical considerations must be carefully navigated to ensure that these tactics are used responsibly and transparently, preserving consumer trust and integrity in the process.

CHAPTER 7

Psychological Implications of Reverse Psychology

The **psychological implications of reverse psychology** delve deep into the intricate dynamics of human cognition, perception, and behavior, unveiling both the complexities and the potential consequences of employing this subtle yet powerful strategy.

While reverse psychology offers a compelling framework for influencing behavior and shaping perceptions, its application can have profound psychological implications for both individuals and society as a whole.

Among the primary psychological implications of reverse psychology lies in its impact on autonomy and decision-making processes. By presenting options as suggestions rather than commands, practitioners of reverse psychology seek to encourage voluntary compliance while preserving individuals' sense of agency and control.

However, this delicate balance between influence and autonomy can raise questions about the authenticity of individuals' choices and the extent to which they are influenced by external factors.

Moving deep, the use of reverse psychology techniques can evoke strong emotional responses in individuals, ranging from curiosity and intrigue to frustration and defiance.

By tapping into emotions such as fear, desire, or uncertainty, practitioners of reverse psychology can elicit powerful reactions that motivate behavior change and shape perceptions.

However, the emotional intensity of these responses can also lead to unintended consequences, including feelings of manipulation or exploitation.

Moreover, the psychological implications of reverse psychology extend beyond individual interactions to broader societal norms and cultural dynamics. The widespread use of reverse psychology in marketing, advertising, and public discourse can shape social norms and influence collective behavior in significant ways.

For example, the framing of products or services as exclusive or limited in availability can create a sense of urgency and desire that drives consumer demand, shaping market trends and consumer preferences.

Ethical considerations also play a central role in the psychological implications of reverse psychology. While these tactics can be highly effective in influencing behavior, they must be used responsibly and transparently to avoid manipulation or coercion.

Practitioners of reverse psychology must consider the potential impact of their strategies on individuals' autonomy, well-being, and decision-making processes, ensuring that their tactics uphold principles of **integrity**, **honesty**, and **respect** for individuals' dignity.

Furthermore, the psychological implications of reverse psychology can vary depending on cultural differences and social contexts. What may be perceived as persuasive or motivational in one cultural context may be seen as manipulative or coercive in another.

Practitioners must be mindful of these differences and adapt their strategies accordingly, respecting the cultural norms and values of their target audience.

Finally, the psychological implications of reverse psychology are multifaceted and far-reaching, encompassing issues of **autonomy**, **emotional response**, **societal influence**, and ethical responsibility.

While this subtle yet powerful strategy offers compelling opportunities for influencing behavior and shaping perceptions, practitioners must navigate these complexities with care and consideration, ensuring that their tactics uphold principles of integrity, transparency, and respect for individuals' autonomy and well-being.

By understanding and addressing the psychological implications of reverse psychology, practitioners can harness its potential for positive impact while minimizing the risk of unintended consequences.

CHAPTER 8

Future Trends and Innovations in Reverse Psychological Strategies

Future trends and innovations in reverse psychological strategies are poised to leverage the remarkable capabilities of the human mind, ushering in a new era of influence and persuasion that harnesses the power of human physical intellects.

As our understanding of psychology deepens and technology continues to evolve, practitioners of reverse psychology are exploring innovative approaches that tap into the innate strengths of human cognition and perception.

One promising trend in reverse psychology is the integration of neuroscientific insights into persuasion techniques. By studying the underlying neural mechanisms of decision-making and behavior, researchers can identify patterns and neural correlates that inform more targeted and effective persuasion strategies.

For example, neurofeedback interventions that train individuals to regulate their brain activity in response to persuasive messages hold promise for enhancing cognitive control and decision-making skills.

Advancements in cognitive psychology offer new insights into the biases and heuristics that shape human decision-making processes.

By understanding how individuals process information and make choices, practitioners of reverse psychology can develop strategies that appeal to cognitive shortcuts and mental habits.

For instance, framing messages in a way that aligns with individuals' existing beliefs and values can enhance the persuasiveness of communication efforts.

Another emerging trend in reverse psychology is the emphasis on emotional intelligence and empathy in persuasion techniques. By empathizing with individuals' emotional states and understanding their underlying motivations, practitioners can tailor their messages and interventions to resonate more deeply with their target audience.

Techniques such as storytelling, metaphor, and emotional appeals can evoke powerful emotional responses that drive behavior change and shape perceptions.

Moreover, the rise of experiential marketing and immersive storytelling offers new opportunities for practitioners of reverse psychology to engage with audiences on a visceral level.

By creating interactive experiences that captivate the senses and evoke emotional responses, marketers can forge deeper connections with consumers and foster brand loyalty.

From augmented reality (AR) experiences to interactive installations, these innovative approaches leverage the power of human perception and imagination to influence behavior and shape attitudes.

In addition, future trends in reverse psychology are likely to be shaped by shifting societal values and cultural norms. As individuals become increasingly conscious of the persuasive tactics used in marketing and advertising, there is a growing demand for transparency, authenticity, and ethical responsibility in communication practices.

Practitioners of reverse psychology must adapt their strategies accordingly, prioritizing honesty, integrity, and respect for individuals' autonomy and well-being.

In conclusion, future trends and innovations in reverse psychological strategies hold promise for unlocking the full potential of human physical intellects in influencing behavior and shaping perceptions. By integrating insights from neuroscience, cognitive psychology, and emotional intelligence, practitioners can develop more sophisticated and effective strategies for persuasion that resonate with their target audience on a profound level.

Whether in marketing, healthcare, education, or public policy, the principles of reverse psychology offer endless possibilities for creating positive change and fostering meaningful connections in an increasingly complex and interconnected world.

By embracing these future trends and innovations, practitioners can harness the power of human intellects to inspire, empower, and transform lives for the better.

CONCLUSION

The landscape of reverse psychology is continually evolving, driven by advancements in our understanding of human cognition and behavior.

As practitioners explore new approaches and techniques, the future of reverse psychological strategies holds immense promise for shaping perceptions, influencing behavior, and fostering meaningful connections in a rapidly changing world.

By leveraging insights from neuroscience, cognitive psychology, and emotional intelligence, practitioners can tap into the innate capabilities of the human mind to create more targeted and effective persuasion strategies.

From neurofeedback interventions to experiential marketing experiences, the future of reverse psychology promises to harness the full potential of human physical intellects to inspire, empower, and transform lives for the better.

However, as we embrace these future trends and innovations, it is essential to remain mindful of the ethical implications of reverse psychology. Transparency, authenticity, and respect for individuals' autonomy must guide our practices, ensuring that our strategies uphold principles of integrity and responsibility.

Ultimately, the future of reverse psychology is defined by our commitment to understanding and respecting the complexities of human cognition and behavior.

By embracing innovation, collaboration, and ethical responsibility, practitioners can harness the power of reverse psychology to create positive change and foster meaningful connections in an increasingly interconnected world.